EP Language Arts 2
Printables

This book belongs to:

_____

This book was made for your convenience. It is available for printing from the Easy Peasy All-in-One Homeschool website. It contains all of the printables from Easy Peasy's Language Arts 2 course. The instructions for each page are found in the online course.

Please note, in the various places where parts of speech are practiced, certain words can be categorized in more than one place (you can go for a swim [noun] or you can swim [verb]). If your child marks one of them differently than the answer key indicates, have a conversation with them to find out why.

Easy Peasy All-in-One Homeschool is a free online homeschool curriculum providing high quality education for children around the globe. It provides complete courses for preschool through high school graduation. For EP's curriculum visit allinonehomeschool.com.

EP Language Arts 2 Printables

ISBN-13: 978-1542665445
ISBN-10: 1542665442

First Edition: January 2017

Following Directions

Practice following the directions in each box. (NOTE: these worksheets must be used with the ONLINE course. They are NOT complete on their own.)

Draw a big number 8. Give it a silly face.	Color one bow tie blue. Color the other bow tie orange and give it a crazy pattern. 
Fill each petal with a different design. You can make your own or use these: stripes, polka dots, zig zags, hearts, and stars. 	Draw 3 different shapes. Color them all differently.

Writing

Describe what tongs look like. Start with "I think tongs look like" and then finish the sentence. Remember to start with a capital letter and end with a period.

_____

_____

_____

_____

_____

_____

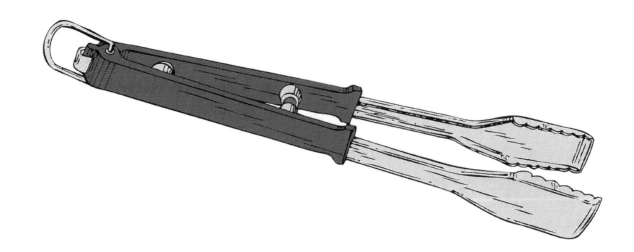

Writing

Write a sentence telling people to be kind to animals. Don't forget a capital letter at the beginning and a period at the end.

_____

_____

_____

_____

_____

Writing

Write a sentence that doesn't make any sense! Here's an example: I drank hamburgers for breakfast. If you need more help you can see the examples at the bottom of the page.

_____

_____

_____

_____

_____

I saw veggies waving as they ran.

A penguin painted my portrait.

The cupcake gave me a balloon.

My flower made a funny face.

Writing

Write a short story. Here's the beginning: I was pulling weeds in my garden and noticed something unusual sticking up out of the dirt.

_____

_____

_____

_____

_____

_____

_____

_____

_____

_____

Writing

Copy these lines of a poem: *The cat she walks on padded claws.*
The wolf on the hills lays stealthy paws.

_____

_____

_____

Ordering Directions

Put these directions for making a peanut butter and jelly sandwich in order using the words in the box.

| first | second | third | fourth | fifth | then | finally |

_____ Spread the peanut butter
on the bread.

_____ Open the jelly.

_____ Enjoy your lunch!

_____ Put both pieces of
bread together.

_____ Spread the jelly on
the peanut butter.

_____ Open the peanut
butter.

_____ Gather the bread, peanut
butter, jelly, and knife.

Writing

Copy this sentence: *My clothes are soft and warm, fold upon fold, but I'm so sorry for the poor out in the cold.*

_____

_____

_____

_____

_____

Which two words in the sentence above rhyme?

_____   _____

Writing

Copy these lines of a poem: *If all were sun and never rain,*
                              There'd be no rainbow still.

_____

_____

_____

Capitalization and Punctuation

Underline the words in each sentence that need to be capitalized. Then fill in the punctuation mark that best fits each sentence.

i'm so excited for thanksgiving

would you like to go to central park

what is your favorite food from taco bell

help

what is your favorite christmas song

my november birthday is on a saturday this year

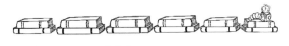
Writing

Copy this line from a poem by Christina Rossetti: *Stroke a flint, and there is nothing to admire: Strike a flint, and forthwith flash out sparks of fire.*

_____

_____

_____

_____

_____

Which two words in the poem above rhyme?

_____   _____

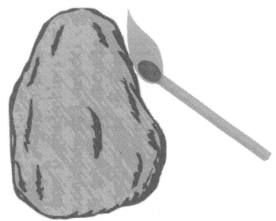

Writing

Finish this sentence with a rhyme: *If a pig wore a wig,* _____. What are some words that rhyme with wig? *big, dig, fig, gig, jig…* Here's an example: *If a pig wore a wig, I'd eat a fig.* If you want to, you can draw a picture of your rhyme in the box.

_____

_____

_____

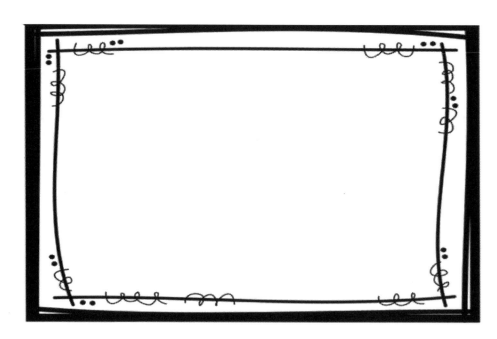

Writing

Copy these two lines of poem by Christina Rossetti:

What will you give me for my pound?
Full twenty shillings round.

_____

_____

_____

Spelling

Remember that **plural** means more than one. Many times a plural word involves an "s" (bikes, toys, balls). Some words don't change form when they are made plural. Copy the word on the line beside it. These are all words that are the same when they are singular (one) or plural (more than one).

deer _____   salmon _____

offspring_____   sheep _____

moose _____   fish _____

Here are two words that are always plural:

scissors _____   pants _____

Writing

Write two lines of a poem like this poem:

What is white? a swan is white
Sailing in the light
What is yellow? pears are yellow,
Rich and ripe and mellow.
What is green? the grass is green,
With small flowers between.

You can use any color you want (blue is easy to rhyme.) If you chose blue, you would start it **What is blue?** Then answer the question and write a rhyme.

_____

_____

_____

_____

Can you think of rhymes for these color words?

pink _____   red _____

black _____   brown _____

white _____   gray _____

Rhyming

Circle the rhyming words in this poem by Christina Rossetti. Underline the words that repeat.

Fly away, fly away over the sea,
Sun-loving swallow, for summer is done;
Come again, come again, come back to me,
Bringing the summer and bringing the sun.

Write two poem lines. Start each line with a repeating phrase and rhyme the last words. For instance: *Summer's here, summer's here, let's go and <u>play</u>.*
Winter's come, winter's come, inside we'll <u>stay</u>.

Make up your own poem or copy the line *Summer's here, summer's here, let's go and play* and then write your own last line. Make sure it rhymes with *play*!

_____

_____

_____

_____

_____

_____

(This page left intentionally blank)

Writing

Copy the first stanza of this poem by Christina Rossetti.

Boats sail on the rivers,
And ships sail on the seas;
But clouds that sail across the sky
Are prettier far than these.

_____

_____

_____

_____

Here are some plurals that don't follow any rules. Cut them out, mix them up, flip them over, then try to match the word to its plural.

ox	oxen	child	children
woman	women	mice	mouse
person	people	tooth	teeth

(This page left intentionally blank)

Writing

Copy this sentence: *Now it is a very unusual thing for Mr. Toad to hurry, very unusual indeed.*

_____

_____

_____

Now write a sentence in the same format. Keep the beginning the same, but add in your own word and then tell about it. Then write a comma, "very" and then your word and then "indeed." *It is a very _____ thing _____, very _____ indeed.*

_____

_____

_____

Writing

Copy this sentence: *You know Peter is always ready to go anywhere or do anything that will satisfy his curiosity.*

_____

_____

_____

Now write a sentence in the same format. Copy the sentence below, filling in the blanks as you copy it. *You know _____ is always ready to _____ or do anything that will _____ .*

_____

_____

_____

Singular and Plural nouns

A noun is *singular* when it refers to only one person, place, thing, or idea:

apple

kid

flower

bee

A noun is *plural* when it refers to more than one person, place, thing, or idea:

apples

kids

flowers

bees

The regular plural form of a noun is made by simply adding an **s** to the end of the word. The following list is a mix of singular and plural nouns. If the noun is in the singular form, write its plural form in the blank. If the noun is in the plural form, write its singular form in the blank.

horse _____   balls _____

faces _____   book _____

shirt _____   clock _____

doors _____   game _____

Write four plural nouns from your reading today or another book you've read.

_____   _____   _____   _____

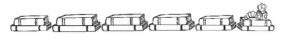

Writing

Copy this sentence: *He envies the birds because they can pour out in beautiful song the joy that is in them.*

_____

_____

_____

Now write a sentence in the same format. Write *Sometimes I envy*, then write a kind of animal, then write *because*, and then write what they can do that you wish you could do.

_____

_____

_____

Plural Rules

The regular plural of nouns is made by adding an S to the end of the word. But there are exceptions to this rule. We call these exceptions **irregular plurals**.

We make the plural of nouns that end in CH, SH, X, or SS by adding ES.

one dress two dresses   one fox two foxes   one couch two couches

We make the plural of some nouns that end in F or FE by changing the F or FE to V and adding ES.

one leaf two leaves   one elf two elves

We make the plural of nouns that end in Y not following a vowel by changing the Y to I and adding ES.

one cherry two cherries   one fly two flies

And of course, there are many words that just don't follow a rule.

one woman, two women   one child, two children
one sheep, two sheep   one cactus, two cacti

Write the plurals:

knife _____   boy _____

wish _____   miss _____

try _____   man _____

inch _____   hand _____

box _____   girl _____

loaf _____   pie _____

Writing

Copy the sentence below. Make sure you copy the " " (quotation marks) and the ? (question mark).

"What was the use of wasting my breath?" demanded Old Mr. Toad.

_____

_____

_____

Now it's your turn to write a question. Be sure to use a question mark.

_____

_____

_____

Writing

Copy the sentence below. Make sure you copy all of the , (commas) and ! (exclamation points).

Oh, my, no! No indeed!

_____

_____

_____

Now it's your turn to write a sentence of your own that ends in an exclamation point.

_____

_____

_____

Writing

Copy these sentences. Make sure you copy all of the " (quotation marks) and the ' (apostrophe) and the ? (question mark) and the . (period).

"I'm just watching my babies. Aren't they lovely?" said he.

_____

_____

_____

Now it's your turn to write a sentence of your own that ends in a question mark.

_____

_____

_____

Writing

Copy this sentence. *"Why, I couldn't do that!" he exclaimed right out loud.*

_____

_____

_____

Now it's your turn to write a sentence like the one above. Here's an example: *"I can't believe it!" I shouted.* Write yourself exclaiming something. Use *"* (quotation marks) and ! (exclamation point) and then write who said it. Use the examples. See if you can do it!

_____

_____

_____

Fishing for Nouns

A **noun** is a person (Jeffrey, boy, sister), place (post office, church, Chicago), thing (ball, dog, computer), or idea (love, fear, happiness). Circle the fish below that contain nouns.

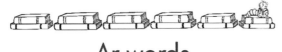
Ar words

Fill in the missing "ar" word using the word box below.

arm	dark	yard	far	barn
car	bark	harp	cart	park

I went out into the _ _ _ _ to play.

We filled our _ _ _ _ at the store.

My dog likes to _ _ _ _ at the TV.

The swings at the _ _ _ _ are fun.

The _ _ _ _ makes a pretty sound.

My grandmother lives _ _ _ away.

The hayloft is in the _ _ _ _.

My sister is afraid of the _ _ _ _.

His _ _ _ was in a sling.

My mom drives a red _ _ _.

Er sound

Fill in the missing "er" word using the word box below. Then write more "er" words on the blank at the bottom.

| serve | skirt | burp | curve | every | blur | turkey | squirrel |

The _ _ _ _ _ _ _ _ ran up the tree.

She had flowers on her _ _ _ _ _.

I _ _ _ _ when I drink soda.

The sign marked the _ _ _ _ _ in the road.

The _ _ _ _ _ _ was delicious.

The cars went so fast they were a

_ _ _ _.

My mother likes to _ _ _ _ _ us dinner.

I brush my teeth _ _ _ _ _ day.

Proper Nouns

Proper nouns are names of people, places, things and ideas. Read the story below. Circle the proper nouns and then write them on the lines below the story. Make sure to capitalize them on the lines!

My favorite day of the week is friday. I start the day with my favorite cereal, choco chunkies. It's a special treat I only get to have on that day. Then I find all of my library books from the previous week, since it's the day we get to go to central library and pick out new books. I love reading and finding new stories! That afternoon, we get to have lunch at my favorite sandwich shop, anderson's deli. The sandwich I get is called monster cheese. It's so warm and toasty and delicious. That evening is basketball practice. This year, my team is the crushers, and my dad is the coach. I'm on the team with my best friend, james. Finally, when I fall into bed after a long day, it's always nice to realize the next day is saturday, so I can just relax!

1. _____

2. _____

3. _____

4. _____

5. _____

6. _____

7. _____

8. _____

Spelling

Write as many words as you can that have the "or" sound and are spelled with OR. You can use the pictures to help you come up with ideas. Rhyming the words will help you come up with more.

1. _____

2. _____

3. _____

4. _____

5. _____

6. _____

7. _____

8. _____

Spelling

Write these words that make the "i" sound in a different way: *fire, pie, dial, pile, light, bicycle, by, bye, guide.*

_____

_____

_____

A tisket, a tasket, a noun in a basket. Circle the baskets that contain the nouns.

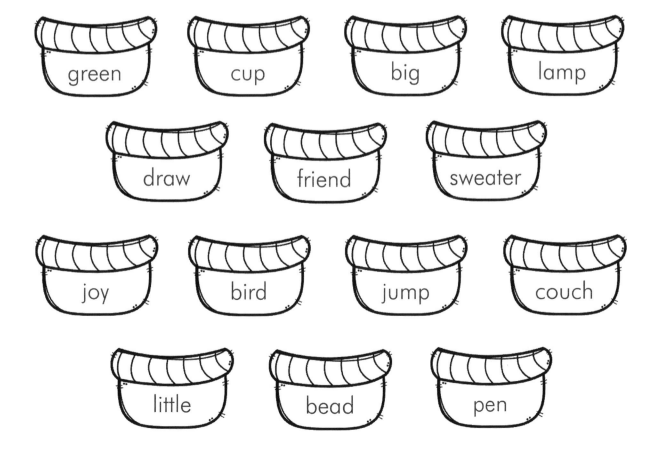

Spelling

Write words that rhyme with bare and are spelled the same way. They should all end in –are. (Here's one to start you off: scare).

1. _____   4. _____

2. _____   5. _____

3. _____   6. _____

Circle the baskets that contain proper nouns.

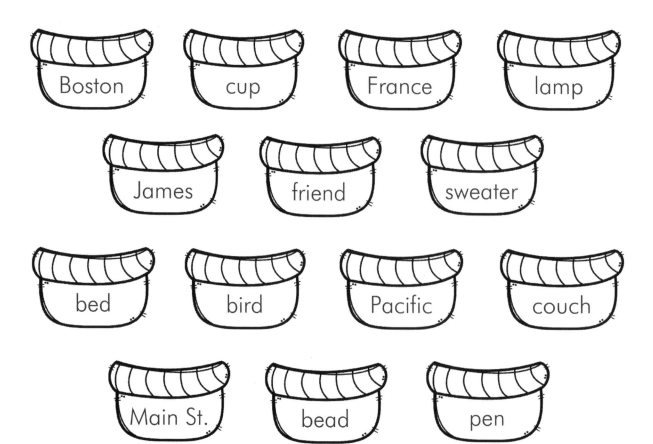

Boston   cup   France   lamp

James   friend   sweater

bed   bird   Pacific   couch

Main St.   bead   pen

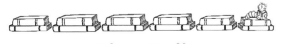

Play Ball

Help the basketball player choose the right balls for his game. Color orange the basketballs that have the same vowel sound as . Choose one of the words to write on the blank at the bottom of the page.

fair

floor

mist

trash

hair

cheer

stair

ball

fear

air

_____

Different Nouns

A **noun** is a person, place, thing or idea. A **proper noun** names a *specific* person, place, thing or idea. Since they are names, proper nouns are always capitalized.

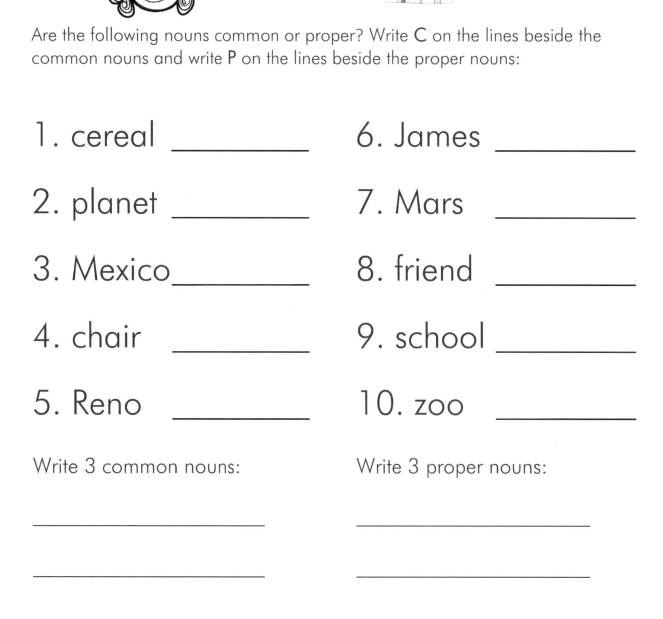

Carol   Calvary

A **common noun** is a *general* person, place, thing or idea. Since they are not names, common nouns are only capitalized if they begin a sentence.

girl   church

Are the following nouns common or proper? Write **C** on the lines beside the common nouns and write **P** on the lines beside the proper nouns:

1. cereal _____   6. James _____

2. planet _____   7. Mars _____

3. Mexico _____   8. friend _____

4. chair _____   9. school _____

5. Reno _____   10. zoo _____

Write 3 common nouns: Write 3 proper nouns:

_____   _____

_____   _____

_____   _____

Oy!

Find the hidden toy! Color red all of the spaces with words that have the same vowel sound as "toy." Color the rest of the words brown.

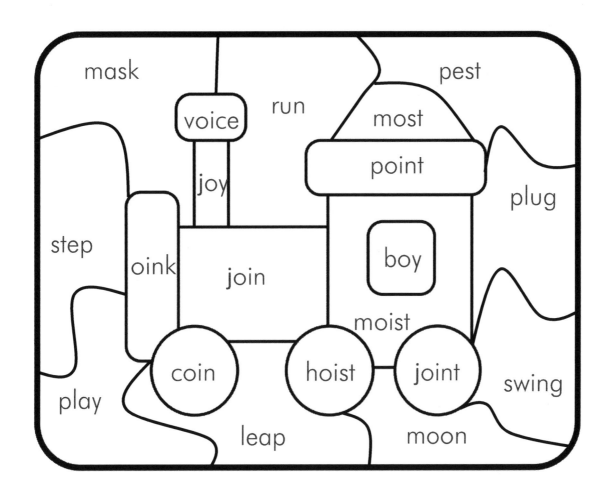

mask

voice

run

pest

most

point

joy

plug

step

oink

join

boy

moist

coin

hoist

joint

swing

play

leap

moon

Write your name, phone number, and address:

Name: _____   Phone: _____

Address: _____

Crossword – Ow sound

Fill in the correct word from the word box to complete the crossword puzzle.

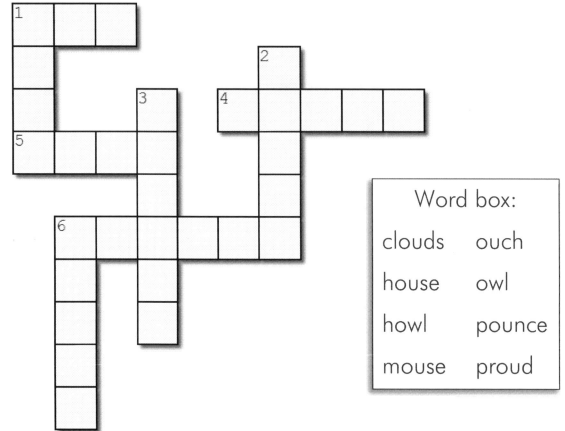

Word box:

clouds   ouch

house   owl

howl   pounce

mouse   proud

Across
1. The _____ was hooting in the trees.
4. The _____ ate all of the cheese.
5. Our dog will sometimes _____ at the door.
6. Some cats love to _____.

Down
1. When I fell off my bike, I screamed, "_____!"
2. Our _____ is the smallest on our street.
3. The sky was full of _____.
6. I am _____ when I work hard.

Circle the common nouns and underline the proper nouns:

cat   Utah   fast   tree   big   Pete   pail   face

eat   brick   Jane   meal   wall   pink   Earth

Aw sound

Use the words from the box to fill in the blanks. Then draw a picture of one of the sentences or draw your own "aw" scene.

| saw | paw | cause | draw | pause | flaw |

My dog licked his _____.

I love to _____ pictures.

We had to _____ the movie.

My biggest _____ is a lack of patience.

I _____ a deer in the backyard.

She's raising money for a good _____.

AL words

Use the words from the box to fill in the blanks. Then find them in the word search. Finally, write 3 words that rhyme with the words from the box.

| fall | walked | hall | call | all | tall |

I heard my mom _____ for me so I _____ down the _____. I tripped over a toy and had quite the _____. I needed a bandage for my knee. Thankfully, I am _____ because they were on the top shelf. As my little sister would say, the bandage made it _____ better.

```
F A T A L L C T L
A C N Q D Z A R A
L R G I F T L Y L
L H A L L A L P L
B W A L K E D Z X
```

Nouns

Circle the common nouns and underline the proper nouns. Then write five common nouns and five proper nouns in the blanks at the bottom.

1. Jessica and Andrew went to Matthew's house.

2. The boys all ran around Northgate Mall.

3. The girls played with the ball at Griffith Park.

4. Maya loved to dress up her doll.

5. Kate had some cake.

6. The book belonged to Jack.

7. Henry was Central Zoo's biggest tortoise.

8. There was a loud noise in the backyard.

Common nouns:

1. _____

2. _____

3. _____

4. _____

5. _____

Proper nouns:

1. _____

2. _____

3. _____

4. _____

5. _____

Story Order

Read the story below. Then put the pictures in the order they happened in the story by numbering the boxes. Finally, underline the 5 words in the story that have the long a sound.

During the week, I do a lot of the same things. I wake up in the morning and make my bed. I have breakfast and then start my school work. I'm usually done by lunch time. After lunch, I love to ride my bike. It's good exercise and a lot of fun. I also like to build things and try to figure out how things work. At the end of a long day, I love to relax in the bathtub. What does your daily schedule look like?

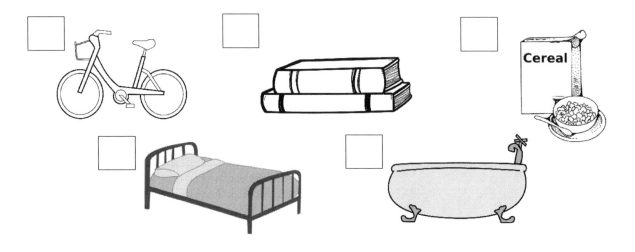

Ing words

Each of the pictures represents a word that ends in **ing**. Write the word beside the picture it represents. Then write four sentences using ing words.

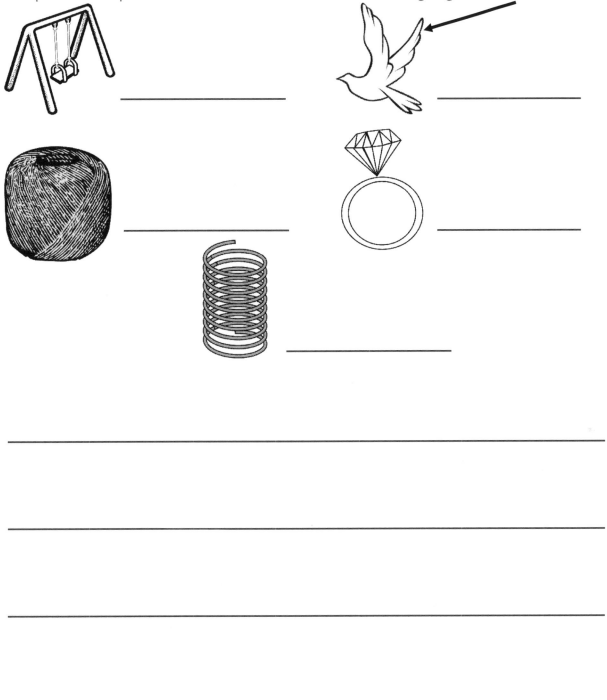

Ink sound

Fill in the blank with the "ink" word from the box that best fits the description.

| think rink ink drink brink stink sink |
| pink wink blink mink |

What a skunk has _____

When I close my eyes fast _____

What's inside a pen _____

What I do with my brain _____

What I do with milk _____

Put these sentences in the correct order.

| going   park   She   brother.   with   to   her   the   is |

_____

_____

| coming,   excited!   and   cousin   I'm   is   so   My |

_____

_____

Ank sound

Fill in the missing "ank" words below.

| bank | thank | drank | sank | crank | stank | plank | rank |

After the skunk sprayed, the air _____.

I _____ some milk.

My heart _____ when I heard the news.

I always say please and _____ you.

The deck had a loose _____ of wood.

We got some money at the _____.

When I _____ my favorite colors, red is number one.

The old fashioned ice cream maker had a hand _____.

Write a sentence using **smug** or **envious**. Examples: *She thought she was the best swimmer ever and was so* **smug** *about it. She was* **envious** *of how well the other girls could swim.*

_____

_____

Noun Review

Underline all the nouns in each sentence.

The girls played with their dolls in the playroom.

The boys kicked the ball in the backyard.

Samuel read a book in his bed.

The phone rang and woke up Jan.

Write **P** for proper or **C** for common in the blank beside each noun.

book _____   James _____

Chicago_____   sock _____

Jupiter _____   love _____

Write the plural of each word in the blank beside it.

finger _____   cup _____

lamp _____   picture _____

flower _____   friend _____

Write a sentence using **amble** or **hastily**. Examples: *He **ambled** down the street whistling a tune. He **hastily** ate breakfast and spilled his juice.*

_____

_____

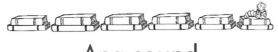

Ang sound

Fill in the blanks with the "ang" word that best fits. Then put the pictures in the order of the story by numbering the boxes.

sang   rang   bang   hang

The phone _____ and woke me up. It was my Aunt Cathy. She _____ Happy Birthday to me. I sat straight up in bed and tried not to _____ my head on the wall. I told my aunt, "Don't _____ up, but my birthday is next week!" We had a good laugh.

Write a sentence using **indignant** or **scornfully**. Examples: *She was* **indignant** *that someone would step on her foot. She looked at the bread* **scornfully** *and said, "I would never eat that!"*

_____

_____

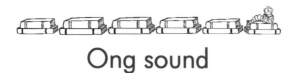

Ong sound

Color orange all of the words in the puzzle that rhyme with "song." Color the rest of the words blue.

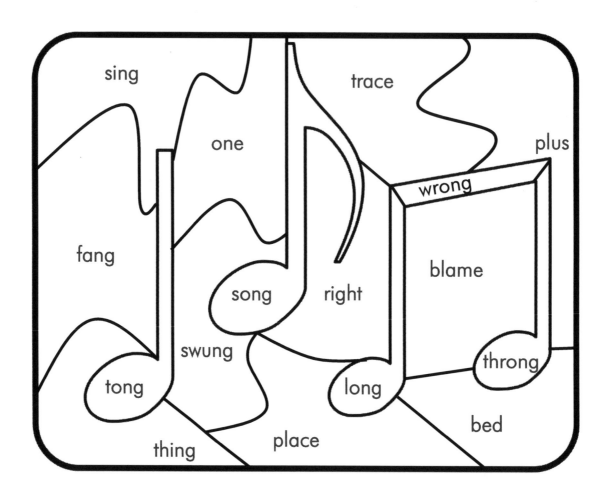

Write a sentence using **anxious** or **feeble**. Examples: *The big storm made him anxious. He has been sick for so long he has become* **feeble**.

_____

_____

Ung sound

Fill in the "ung" words that best fit the blanks below. Then write 3 more sentences about what the girl does at home.

| sung | rung | hung | swung | flung |

A girl _____ from the monkey bars at the playground. As she _____ there, she thought of the song they had _____ in choir about a monkey swinging through the trees. When she climbed down the ladder, her shoe got stuck on a _____. "Maybe I wouldn't make a very good monkey," she thought as she _____ herself down.

_____

_____

_____

_____

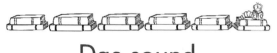
Dge sound

Fill in the "dge" words that best fit the blanks below. One is a proper noun! If you want to, you can color the pictures that correspond to the sentences.

Pledge   edge   badge   fudge   lodge

I earned a _____ in my

scout program.

I love to make peppermint

_____ with my mom.

We stayed at the _____

when we went on vacation.

I saw a rainbow at the

_____ of the clouds.

We said the _____ of

Allegiance.

Write a sentence about anything you want. Remember how to start and finish it.

_____

_____

Word Scramble

Unscramble the letters to make words that end with the same ending as .

tfyif   _____

ydnca   _____

npoy   _____

byab   _____

yenmo   _____

50

Write a sentence about anything you want. Remember how to start and finish it.

_____

_____

Le ending

Fill in the "le" words that best fit the blanks below. Use the pictures if you need help figuring out the word. You can color the pictures if you want to.

We lit a _____ when the power went out.

My favorite snack is an _____ with peanut butter.

My baby brother loves to drink his _____.

My pet _____ is named Myrtle.

We eat at the dining room _____.

Write a question. What punctuation mark belongs at the end?

_____

_____

Ea words

All of the pencils have "ea" words on them, but they have different sounds!
Color red the words that have the same vowel sound as red. Color gray the
words that have the same vowel sound as gray.

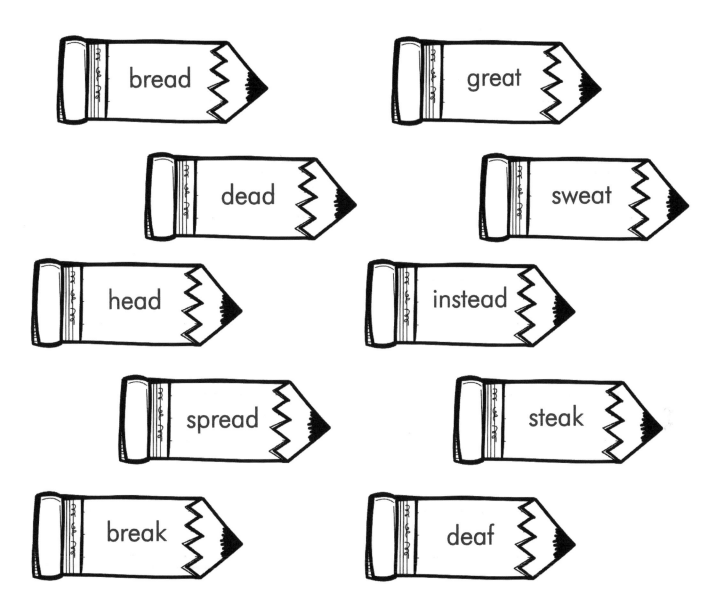

How many red pencils are there? _____

How many gray pencils are there? _____

(This page left intentionally blank)

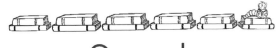

Ou words

Each basket has a word on it. Cut and paste the balloons with the same vowel sound onto the strings coming out of that basket.

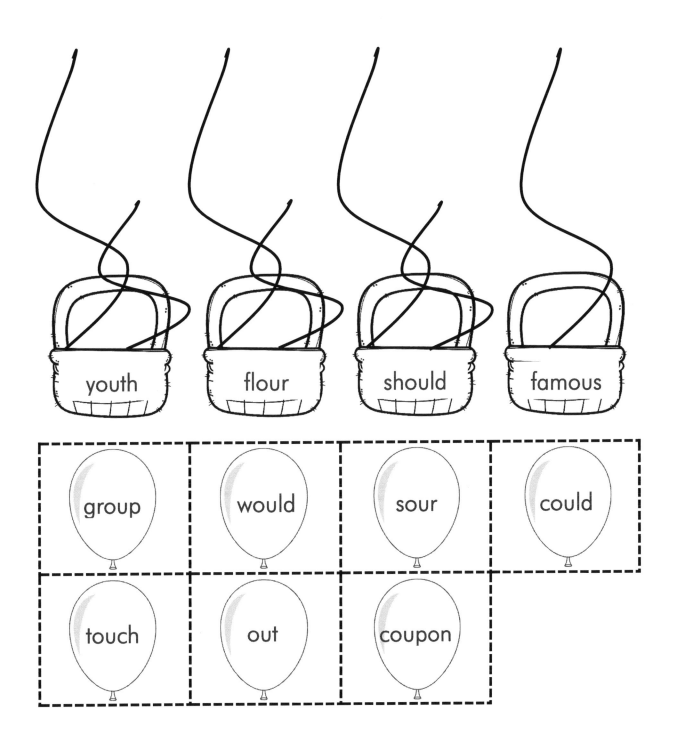

(This page left intentionally blank)

Plural Review

Fill in the plural of each word in the blank beside the word. For many nouns, you simply add an "s" to make it plural. Here are some reminders about the exceptions:

For nouns that end in ch, sh, x, o, or ss, add "es."
For some nouns ending in f or fe, change those endings to "ves."
For nouns that end in a consonant followed by a y, change the y to "ies."
For some nouns that have oo, change oo to "ee."
Many other irregular nouns don't follow any rule: children, deer, men, etc.

foot _____   toy _____

itch _____   elf _____

baby _____   woman_____

fox _____   ball _____

hero _____   deer _____

kiss _____   hug _____

goose_____   knife _____

candy_____   box _____

Oo Crossword

Use the pictures to fill in the crossword puzzle. All of the words have "oo" in them.

Across:

2.

4.

5.

Down:

1.

3.

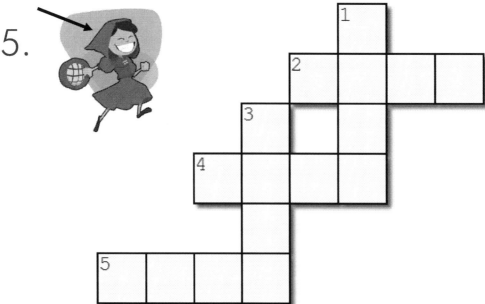

Writing

Copy this sentence: *He stopped and into his yellow eyes crept a look of suspicion.*

_____

_____

Fill in the blanks with either "gh" or "ph" to make the missing "f" sound. Match the words to the pictures.

___one

___oto

ele___ant

lau___

rou___

Writing

Underline the silent letters in the words that contain them below. Then find those words in the picture. Finally, write them on the lines at the bottom.

two   big   knife   dog   comb   sign   wave   man

_____

_____

Spelling

Copy these words that have the "oi" sound in them: *oil, boil, coin, noise, noisy, avoid, choice, point*.

_____

_____

_____

_____

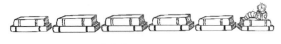
Writing

Write a sentence using at least two words from your spelling list on lesson 67. Here are the words again: *oil, boil, coin, noise, noisy, avoid, choice, point*. Here are examples: *I made the choice to avoid all noisy coins. When oil boils, its noise is noisy.* Make sure your sentences start with a capital letter and end with punctuation!

_____

_____

_____

_____

Writing

Copy this part of a sentence: *Jimmy Skunk was smiling as he ambled towards the old house of Johnny Chuck.* Make sure you make their names start with capital letters. Names are always capitalized.

_____

_____

_____

Parts of Speech

You know that a **noun** is a person, place, thing, or idea. Choose a noun from this list: boy, girl, house, tree, chair.

An **adjective** is a word that describes a noun. Choose an adjective from this list: green, big, striped, happy, tired.

A **verb** is an action word that tells what the noun is doing. Choose a verb from this list: laughing, running, jumping, eating, sleeping.

Now draw a picture that illustrates all three words together.

Writing

Try to write this sentence in proper English. Read it out loud to help you figure out what it says: *Ah have mo' important things to worry about.*

_____

_____

_____

Verbs

Remember that verbs show action. Can you find 10 verbs in the words below? Circle them, or color them if you'd like.

Writing

Copy this sentence: *Buster Bear could squash me by just stepping on me, but he doesn't try it.*

_____

_____

_____

_____

Plurals

Write the plural in the blank beside each word.

place _____   tax _____

match_____   lady _____

mess _____   wife _____

Action Verbs

Each line contains one action verb. Circle it.

1. paper   snow   sheet   flying

2. watching   note   brother   bag

3. green   hair   write   cheek

4. cheer   wagon   lamp   tissue

5. chair   sit   tooth   shorts

6. noise   loud   shout   ear

7. library   book   quiet   read

8. giggle   happy   smiley   mouth

9. couch   kneel   shirt   floor

10. ice   water   shoes   type

Writing

Write about your birthday.

_____

_____

_____

_____

_____

_____

_____

_____

Writing

Write about your favorite thing to do. Why do you like it?

_____

_____

_____

_____

_____

_____

_____

_____

_____

Verb Types

Every sentence has a subject (a person or a thing) and a verb. Circle the subject and underline the verb in each of the following sentences.

1. Rebecca painted a beautiful picture.

2. The ball rolled down the hill.

3. I dropped my book.

4. God's creation is magnificent.

5. Mr. Anderson teaches math.

The main verb in a sentence either shows action (**action verbs**) or a state of being (**linking verbs**). Write an A next to the action verbs and an L next to the linking verbs below.

yell _____   are _____

leap _____   want _____

is _____   slept _____

be _____   was _____

Writing

Write a short story about what you would do if you saw a skunk. You can start it something like this: *"I was taking a walk when all of a sudden a skunk ambled out onto the path in front of me."* Then what happened?

_____

_____

_____

_____

_____

_____

_____

_____

_____

_____

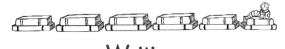

Writing

Write a short story about what you would do if you could be invisible.

_____

_____

_____

_____

_____

_____

_____

_____

_____

_____

_____

Find the Verbs

Uncover the hidden picture! If the word is a verb, color the space orange. If it is not a verb, color the space gray.

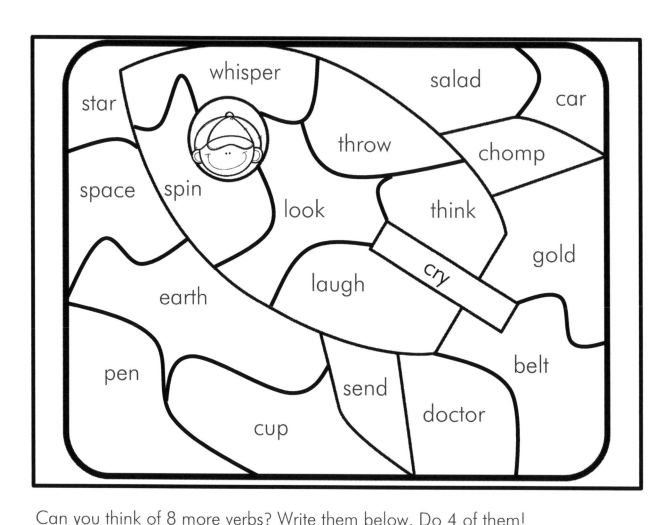

Can you think of 8 more verbs? Write them below. Do 4 of them!

_____   _____

_____   _____

_____   _____

_____   _____

Action Verbs

Remember that action verbs tell what someone or something does. They show action. Circle the action verbs in each of the sentences below.

Show me your picture.

Clean up your room.

Can I come?

He hit the ball.

We honked the horn.

Can we go home?

She ran away.

Play verb charades! Cut or tear a scrap paper into 10 pieces. Write 10 verbs on the pieces. Put them into a bag and take turns with your family drawing a slip of paper and acting out the verb without talking. Try to guess each others' verbs!

To Be

The verb *to be* is a verb that shows a state of being. Use the chart to fill in the missing form of *to be* in each sentence.

Person	Past	Present	Future
I	was	am	will be
you, they, we	were	are	will be
he, she, it	was	is	will be

Uncle Bob _____ home, but now he's not.

The ball _____ flat now since it hit a nail.

Tomorrow it _____ hot.

Yesterday it _____ cold.

I _____ going to the store later.

They _____ loud, but now they _____ quiet.

It _____ a beautiful day, isn't it?

You _____ coming over later.

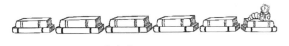

Writing

Write a sentence that is a question. What punctuation mark should go at the end? Then write an answer that is an exclamation. What punctuation mark should go at the end?

_____

_____

_____

_____

_____

Circle the flowers that contain linking verbs.

Linking Verbs

Circle the linking verbs in the sentences below. Some of them aren't in the "to be" form. One sentence has an action verb in it. Can you find it? Underline it.

My dad is an architect.

The mail will be delayed tomorrow.

The girls were tired after their soccer game.

The girl seems shy.

I went to the store yesterday.

It was very windy today.

My dog looks hungry.

Your turn! Write two sentences with linking verbs. Circle your linking verbs.

_____

_____

_____

_____

Verbs

Find and write five linking verbs and five action verbs from something you've read recently. Remember, every sentence has a verb!

Linking Verbs

_____

_____

_____

_____

_____

Action Verbs

_____

_____

_____

_____

_____

(This page left intentionally blank)

Matching

Cut out the squares, mix them up and lay them face down on the table. Play a matching game where you match the sentences to either the **past tense** (already happened) or **future tense** (will happen later) of the verb in parentheses at the bottom.

We ____ cards last night. (play)	played	We ____ golf next week. (play)	will play
We ____ up the answer when we weren't sure. (look)	looked	Later tonight we ____ at the stars. (look)	will look
Last Christmas I ____ most of my relatives. (see)	saw	We ____ the new movie when it comes out. (see)	will see

Copy this sentence: *"The bride looked like a queen."* Do you think that's a nice way to describe her? Is it better than saying she looked pretty? What image do you picture?

_____

_____

(This page left intentionally blank)

Past Tense

Verbs in the **past tense** are showing that something already happened. To make most verbs past tense, you simply add "ed" to the end. There are some exceptions to this. Read the examples and then make the verbs past tense.

If a verb ends in e, simply add "d" instead of "ed" (bake = baked).

race _____   please _____

tame _____   fake _____

If a verb ends in a consonant followed by a y, change the y to an i and then add "ed." If it ends in a vowel followed by a y, leave the y and add "ed." This is similar to the plural rule for words ending in y (carry = carried, play = played).

hurry _____   obey _____

cry _____   stay _____

Make these verbs past tense.

place _____   jump _____

dry _____   wash _____

color _____   clean _____

enjoy _____   ask _____

like _____   try _____

guess _____   worry _____

Writing

Write about what you did yesterday. Use the words **first**, **next**, and **last** to start your sentences. That means your story should be in order. What did you do first? What did you do next? What did you do last? Write at least three sentences, starting each one with one of those words.

_____

_____

_____

_____

_____

_____

_____

_____

Writing

Copy this sentence: *"But why do you carry that door?" asked the sheriff.* Make sure you write all of the punctuation. There are quotation marks showing that someone is speaking. There is a question mark showing that he is asking a question. There is a period to end the sentence. Also watch your spelling.

Spelling

Find the **er** words in the puzzle below.

```
H E R D L A W S Y B P R F T J
V M I S T E R E S L Y J N A T
H V B Q T B W S L I W M Z B I
E S I S T E R I C S U O O L S
R M P J A Y D L A T W T F E T
B F A T W A U V I E Z H E S E
A R W L F W S E A R N E R L R
V E R B Y N H R Y U W R N K N
B E F F A T H E R P D Z H E R
```

her	stern	mister
verb	fern	blister
silver	herb	mother
sister	herd	father

(continued on next page)

Spelling

Practice spelling your words! Have someone read you the words from the previous page and try to write them from memory onto the lines below.

Action Verbs

For each sentence, find the action verb and write it in the blank.

We went to the store early Friday morning. _____

We put the groceries into the shopping cart. _____

We had to wait at the checkout for a long time. _____

We finally paid the cashier for our groceries. _____

We then loaded our car with all of the groceries. _____

We carefully drove home for a late lunch. _____

Which word is the action verb in each sentence?

I read the whole book.

a. read   c. whole

b. book   d. the

My dad grilled our burgers.

a. dad   c. burgers

b. my   d. grilled

She sat on the cold bench.

a. cold   c. sat

b. bench   d. on

We went to the beach.

a. beach   c. to

b. went   d. we

The bag hung on the hook.

a. hook   c. hung

b. bag   d. on

The ice cracked in the glass.

a. cracked   c. in

b. ice   d. glass

Linking Verbs

For each sentence, find the linking verb and write it in the blank.

That girl seems nice and friendly to me.   _____

All the kids who came look so happy.   _____

She was so hungry she wanted seconds.   _____

Harold is an award-winning sushi chef.   _____

Her shoes are the muddiest I've ever seen. _____

My dad is thirsty and is asking for iced tea. _____

Which word is the verb in each sentence?

We were late for church.

a. late   c. church

b. we   d. were

My sister has been sick.

a. My   c. has been

b. sister   d. sick

The baby is hungry.

a. the   c. is

b. baby   d. hungry

She feels very cold.

a. She   c. very

b. feels   d. cold

His room was a mess.

a. his   c. mess

b. was   d. room

They will be here tomorrow.

a. tomorrow   c. will be

b. here   d. they

Verb Tense

The verb tense places a verb in time. The three main tenses are **past tense** (already happened), **present tense** (happening right now), and **future tense** (will happen later). Use the chart to help you fill in the right verb for each sentence. If you're having trouble, read the sentence out loud with each choice. The one that sounds right is probably the right one. Put a star next to the sentence in **present tense**.

Past	Present	Future
I baked cupcakes.	I bake cupcakes.	I will bake cupcakes.
I was baking cupcakes.	I am baking cupcakes.	I will be baking cupcakes.
I had been baking cupcakes.	I have been baking cupcakes.	I am going to bake cupcakes.

We _____ to church tomorrow.
(went/will go)

I _____ my bike yesterday.
(rode/ride)

My sister _____ right now.
(slept/is sleeping)

Yesterday, we _____ pancakes.
(eat/ate)

I _____ God forever.
(followed/will follow)

Writing

Choose three action verbs. They can be any three action verbs you want. Write them in the blanks:

_____   _____   _____

Now write three sentences using your three verbs. Make sure the sentences and the verb tense match!

_____

_____

_____

_____

_____

_____

_____

Verb Tense

Write the correct tense of the action verb to match the rest of the sentence.

(to dig) Yesterday, my dog _____ a hole.

(to sing) I _____ a solo next week.

(to write) I _____ a poem last night.

(to sleep) She _____ right now.

(to play) Later, we _____ outside.

(to cook) Whenever he _____, I eat well.

(to watch) We _____ the game now.

(to run) I _____ a race last week.

(to eat) I _____ too much earlier.

(to sit) Next time, I _____ beside you.

(to kick) Watch! She _____ the ball hard.

(to fly) That bird always _____ at night.

Writing

Copy any sentence from a book you are reading. What is the subject? What did the subject do (what is the predicate)? Make sure to start your sentence with a capital letter and end it with punctuation.

_____

_____

_____

Subjects and Verbs

Circle the subject and underline the verbs in the sentences below.

After breakfast, Justin cleaned the table.

The shy little girl hugged her mom's leg.

The hyper puppy dropped his ball at my feet.

The food was piping hot.

Sandra forgot her flute for band rehearsal.

William ran the ball up the field.

Predicates

The complete **predicate** is anything that isn't the subject — it tells what the subject of the sentence does. Underline the complete predicate in each sentence below.

Riley swept the kitchen.

Andrew rode his bike.

Olivia threw the ball.

The surfer caught the big wave.

The phone rang loudly.

The pig rolled in the mud.

The rainbow appeared over the clouds.

The dishwasher cleaned the dishes.

My mom went to the store.

Writing

There's a story where the ruler, a tyrant, made a law that everyone had to bow down to his hat. Pretend that you are king of a country. Write about what laws you would make.

_____

_____

_____

_____

_____

_____

_____

_____

Spelling

Copy each of the words onto the line beside it. Be sure to spell each word correctly!

bright _____   pull _____

eat _____   push _____

far _____   right _____

fight _____   seen _____

flight _____   sight _____

lost _____   strength_____

might _____   tight _____

pole _____   wire _____

Writing

Copy this sentence. It's a little tricky! *"The man who has made up his mind to win,"* said Napoleon, *"will never say impossible."* Be careful to use commas and quotation marks to show someone is speaking. There are also two capital letters in this sentence.

_____

_____

_____

_____

Linking Verbs

Circle the linking verbs below.

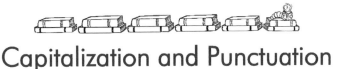

Capitalization and Punctuation

Correct the sentences by underlining the words that should be capitalized and adding any missing punctuation.

my dog is so silly when he chases his tail

mr. robinson was my favorite teacher.

have you ever been to another country

watch out for that patch of ice

we went to alabama last tuesday.

Writing

Copy this sentence. *At first the Romans, who were very proud and brave, did not think there was much danger.* Make sure you use two capital letters and two commas.

_____

_____

_____

_____

Writing

Write a story about the time you ran into a lion.

_____

_____

_____

_____

_____

_____

_____

_____

_____

Spelling

Look at each word, then cover it and try to write it on your own onto the line beside it. Check your spelling and correct any mistakes. These are the same words from lesson 111. Do you remember them?

bright _____   pull _____

eat _____   push _____

far _____   right _____

fight _____   seen _____

flight _____   sight _____

lost _____   strength _____

might _____   tight _____

pole _____   wire _____

Writing

Copy this sentence. *Nearly two thousand years ago there lived in Rome a man whose name was Julius Caesar.* Make sure you use capital letters in the right place and make sure you spell his name correctly.

_____

_____

_____

_____

Action Verbs

Circle the action verbs below.

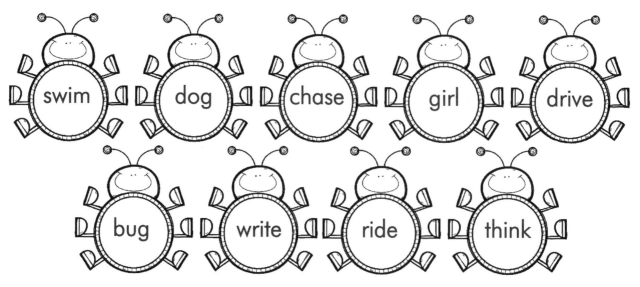

swim   dog   chase   girl   drive

bug   write   ride   think

Ordering Directions

Put these directions for making a snowman in order using the words in the box.

first   second   third   then   finally

_____ Stack the three balls
largest to smallest.

_____ Make the next ball
slightly smaller.

_____ Roll a large ball for the
base of your snowman.

_____ Add eyes, nose,
mouth, and arms.

_____ Make the last ball
the smallest of all.

Put these directions for making scrambled eggs in order using the words in the box.

first   second   third   fourth   fifth   then   finally

_____ Whisk the cracked eggs
and milk in the bowl.

_____ Cook over medium
heat until done.

_____ Serve with toast and
enjoy!

_____ Crack the eggs into
the bowl.

_____ Pour a splash of milk
into the bowl of eggs.

_____ Pour the whisked
eggs into the pan.

_____ Gather the eggs, whisk,
milk, bowl, and pan.

Spelling

Copy each of the words onto the line beside it. Be sure to spell each word correctly!

answer_____   model_____

classify_____   paragraph_____

cough_____   rough _____

dough_____   store _____

enough_____   though_____

glyph _____   tough _____

graph _____   triumph_____

laugh _____   wide _____

Writing

Write the name: **Alexander the Great.**

Possessive Nouns

Choose the noun that shows possession. Things like the dog**'s** bone, the house**'s** door, the girl**'s** hair – these all show possession. Notice the **'s**? Circle the choice that best fits in the blank.

The _____ melody was catchy.
  songs'   song's

The _____ voice was scratchy.
  boy's   boys'

The _____ tire was flat.
  bike's   bikes'

The _____ claws were sharp.
  cats'   cat's

My _____ pages are worn.
  books'   book's

Possessive Nouns

Circle the choice that best fits the blank.

The _____ frosting was delicious.
cupcakes'   cupcake's

The _____ sail was colorful.
boat's   boats'

The _____ laugh was adorable.
baby's   babies'

Writing

Write the name of five people in your family. Now make them each own something by adding 's. For example: *Mom's computer*.

_____

_____

_____

_____

Its/It's

When **it** is possessive, you do not use an apostrophe. When you use an apostrophe in the word, you turn it into a contraction that means "it is." Circle the form of **it** that best fits each sentence. Then write two sentences at the bottom. One should use *its* and mean that something belongs to it. The other should use *it's* and mean it is.

The dog got _____ fur muddy.

    its   it's

_____ really hot outside today.

   Its   It's

I think _____ fun to play in the rain.

    its   it's

_____ house is a hole in the wall.

   Its   It's

_____

_____

_____

_____

Spelling

Look at each word, then cover it and try to write it on your own onto the line beside it. Check your spelling and correct any mistakes. These are the words from lesson 121. Do you remember them?

answer _____   model _____

classify _____   paragraph _____

cough _____   rough _____

dough _____   store _____

enough _____   though _____

glyph _____   tough _____

graph _____   triumph _____

laugh _____   wide _____

Its/It's

Circle the form of **it** that best fits each sentence. Then write two new sentences at the bottom. One should use *its* and mean that something belongs to it. The other should use *it's* and mean it is.

It was so old _____ paint was flaking off.
    its   it's

_____ a beautiful rainbow!
  Its   It's

That's a pretty color. What is _____ name?
    its   it's

_____ Friday today.
  Its   It's

_____

_____

_____

_____

Spelling

Copy each of the words onto the line beside it. Be sure to spell each word correctly!

addition_____   glass_____

confusion_____   key_____

direction _____   location_____

division_____   recreation_____

education_____   sensible_____

explosion_____   subtraction_____

fiction _____   support_____

fig _____   vacation_____

Writing

You are going to write a short story, one sentence at a time. Today, write one sentence with a subject and a predicate. Here are some examples:

I ran home.

My dog ate all the crumbs from around the table.

Someday I'm going to fly away in a hot air balloon.

_____

_____

_____

Writing

Add another sentence to the one you wrote on lesson 132. Just write your new sentence below but make sure it goes with the one you already wrote. In this sentence, use an apostrophe. Here are examples:

I ran home. My sister's bike was lying in the driveway.

My dog ate all the crumbs from around the table. He found the most underneath my brother's high chair.

Someday I'm going to fly away in a hot air balloon. The balloon's name is going to be the *Explorer*.

_____

_____

_____

Writing

Add another sentence to the one you wrote on lesson 133. Just write your new sentence below but make sure it goes with the one you already wrote. Here are examples:

I ran home. My sister's bike was lying in the driveway. I thought I'd take it for a spin.

My dog ate all the crumbs from around the table. He found the most underneath my brother's high chair. My brother is so messy.

Someday I'm going to fly away in a hot air balloon. The balloon's name is going to be the *Explorer*. I think I'll fly it to Africa.

_____

_____

_____

Writing

Add another sentence to the one you wrote on lesson 134. This time you will connect it to the sentence you wrote before using **and**, **but**, or **or**. Take away the punctuation mark from the end of your sentence and write a comma instead. Then write **and**, **but**, or **or** and then your new sentence. Here are examples:

I ran home. My sister's bike was lying in the driveway. I thought I'd take it for a spin, **but** just then she came out of the house and said she was going to ride it.

My dog ate all the crumbs from around the table. He found the most underneath my brother's high chair. My brother is so messy, **and** he loves to throw his food on the floor.

Someday I'm going to fly away in a hot air balloon. The balloon's name is going to be the *Explorer*. I think I'll fly it to Africa, **or** maybe I'll float to Asia.

_____

_____

_____

_____

Spelling

Look at each word, then cover it and try to write it on your own onto the line beside it. Check your spelling and correct any mistakes. These are words from lesson 131. Do you remember them?

addition_____   glass_____

confusion_____   key_____

direction _____   location_____

division_____   recreation_____

education_____   sensible_____

explosion_____   subtraction_____

fiction _____   support_____

fig _____   vacation_____

Subject Pronouns

Use the chart below to fill in the missing subject pronouns from the sentences. (You probably don't even need the chart, but it's there if you do!)

Person	Singular	Plural
1st (speaking)	I	we
2nd (spoken to)	you	you
3rd (spoken about)	he/she/it	they

(Meg, Jill, and I) _____ played ball together.

(Your dad) _____ works hard at his job.

([Speaking to] Tom) _____ are being too loud.

(The dog and cat) _____ chased each other.

(Philadelphia) _____ is a city rich in history.

(You and I) _____ are on the same team.

(Jack and Tom) _____ are on the other team.

(My Aunt Sally) _____ is a nurse.

(The apple) _____ was sweet.

(My brother) _____ likes sweet apples.

Object Pronouns

Use the chart below to fill in the missing object pronouns from the sentences.
(You probably don't even need the chart, but it's there if you do!)

Person	Singular	Plural
1st (speaking)	me	us
2nd (spoken to)	you	you
3rd (spoken about)	him/her/it	them

Brian wanted to play with_____. (Meg, Jill, and me)

You must really love _____.   (Your dad)

I am talking to _____.   ([Speaking to] Tom)

I tried to keep up with _____.   (The dog and cat)

Last year, we visited _____.   (Philadelphia)

The coach seems to like _____.   (You and me)

I hope we don't lose to _____.   (Jack and Tom)

The other nurses really like _____.   (My Aunt Sally)

The orange wasn't sweet like _____.   (The apple)

Apples taste better to _____.   (My brother)

Subject and Object Pronouns

Is the missing pronoun a subject or an object pronoun? Write the correct form of the pronoun in the blank.

I wanted to play with_____, but she was busy.
she/her

You must really love your dad. _____ works hard.
He/Him

I tried to keep up with _____, but they kept running.
they/them

You and I will have fun if the coach puts _____ in.
we/us

Jack and Tom are good. _____ will be hard to beat.
They/Them

My Aunt Sally is kind, so the other nurses like _____.
she/her

My Aunt Sally thinks _____ are kind too.
they/them

My mom went to the store. _____ forgot her list.
She/Her

Writing

Write a sentence with someone's name in it. For example: *Samuel likes to climb walls*. Write a second sentence with a pronoun instead of the name. For example: *He can literally climb up and touch the ceiling*. Now write one last sentence. Use an apostrophe with the name, either showing possession or being used as a contraction. For example: *Samuel's really amazing!* (Samuel is really amazing) or *Samuel's feet are strong to hold him up so high.* (The feet belong to Samuel.) You should have three sentences.

_____

_____

_____

_____

_____

_____

_____

Writing

Write a story about your vacation to a mountain home (pretend). What did you do there? Was it summer or winter?

_____

_____

_____

_____

_____

_____

_____

_____

_____

_____

Writing

Write a story. Start: *He bravely...* or *She bravely...* Then use at least one other word from the word box (from lesson 148). Write at least four sentences. Make sure each of your sentences starts with a capital letter and ends with punctuation.

| bravely | slowly | sadly | cheerful | hopeful |
| fearless | useless | kindness | loudness |

_____

_____

_____

_____

_____

_____

_____

_____

Writing

Copy this sentence: *"I'm afraid I don't know how," replied the country lad.* Pay attention to all of the punctuation and capitalization.

_____

_____

_____

What are the two contractions in the sentence?

_____

What do the contractions mean?

_____

Can you find a pronoun in the sentence?

_____

Can you find a common noun in the sentence?

_____

Writing

Copy this sentence: *"I'll have to teach Danny Rugg a good lesson," said Bert to his cousin.* Pay attention to all of the punctuation and capitalization.

_____

_____

_____

_____

What is the contraction in the sentence?

_____

What does the contraction mean?

_____

Can you find a pronoun in the sentence?

_____

Can you find any proper nouns in the sentence?

_____

Writing

Copy this sentence: *"That's what we'll do!" cried Bert, steering toward it.* Pay attention to all of the punctuation and capitalization.

_____

_____

_____

There is an 's word in the sentence. Is it possessive or a contraction?

_____

What does it mean?

_____

Can you find a pronoun in the sentence?

_____

Can you find a proper noun in the sentence?

_____

Writing

Write sentences like the ones you have been copying. Write what someone is saying and use a contraction. Here are some examples: *"I'll be right there,"* I *said. "He's coming for dinner,"* I told my mom. *"It's time to go!"* I yelled. Write three sentences like the examples.

_____

_____

_____

_____

_____

_____

_____

_____

Writing

Copy this sentence: *By this time the snowslide had reached the tree, and the mass was now much larger than at first.* Can you draw a picture of what is happening?

_____

_____

_____

_____

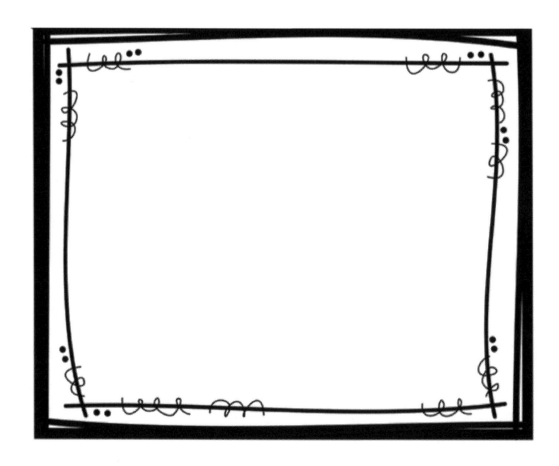

Writing

Copy this sentence: *Then came another thaw, and a freeze followed some days later, making good skating.*

_____

_____

_____

_____

Can you find a plural noun in the sentence?

_____

Can you find the two past tense verbs?

_____

Can you find the present tense verb?

_____

Writing

Think of any place in the world you would like to go. Why would you like to go there? Write about it. Tell where you would like to go and why. What would you do when you got there? How long would you stay?

_____

_____

_____

_____

_____

_____

_____

_____

_____